Garfield

The Incurable Romantic

BY: JIM DAVIS

RR

Ravette London

This edition first published by
Ravette Limited 1986

Printed and bound in Great Britain
for Ravette Limited,
3 Glenside Estate, Star Road, Partridge Green,
Horsham, Sussex RH13 8RA
by William Clowes Limited, Beccles and London.

ISBN 0 948456 32 9

The Incurable Romantic

Valentino has nothing on this romantic feline. Garfield will charm you with his charisma, endear you with his wit and enchant you with his sweet and subtle sensitivity. Well ... two out of three isn't too bad. One thing's for certain, Garfield will have you swooning with laughter as he takes romantic comedy to its hilarious limit.

GARFIELD

ZOO

I WONDER WHAT IT WOULD BE LIKE TO BE A WILD ANIMAL

DO NOT FEED THE ANIMALS

ZOO

FIRST, I'D ALTER THIS STUPID SIGN

DO NOT

FEED THE ANIMALS

THEN I'D PACE AROUND LOOKING KINDA FIERCE

FEED THE ANIMALS

JIM DAVIS   1-16

THEN I'D SCARE THE HECK OUT OF THE CROWD

EEEEK!

SWIPE

THAT WAS A PRETTY CONVINCING PERFORMANCE, IF I DO SAY SO MYSELF

GARFIELD

ISN'T THAT HALLEY'S COMET?!

ZIP!

GARFIELD, DID YOU TAKE MY STEAK?

WHO? LITTLE OL' ME?

JIM DAVIS

1-23

LOOK, I DON'T HAVE YOUR CRUMMY OLD STEAK

HEY! I DON'T HAVE YOUR CRUMMY OLD STEAK!

I'M GOING TO GET YOU FOR THIS, ODIE

BURP

3-6

THIS LOOKS LIKE A GOOD DAY FOR SOME HEAVY THOUGHTS

LET'S PUT THIS WHOLE THING IN PERSPECTIVE

EATING IS IMPORTANT

JIM DAVIS

AND SLEEPING IS IMPORTANT

5-1

© 1983 United Feature Syndicate, Inc.

BUT NOTHING IS MORE IMPORTANT THAN HOLDING SOMEONE YOU LOVE

CHECK THAT

RECIPROCATION IS NICE, TOO

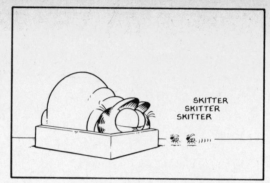

HELLO

YOU CAN TELL A LOT ABOUT A FAMILY FROM THEIR GARBAGE

THEY HAVE AN INFANT WHO JUST OUTGREW ITS BABY CLOTHES

JIM DAVIS

THE FATHER RECENTLY GAVE UP GOLFING

6-26

AND THE MOTHER COOKS LOTS OF PASTA

© 1983 United Feature Syndicate, Inc.

ADOPT ME!

WHAT DO YOU THINK OF MY MING VASE, GARFIELD?

(CRASH!)

MING, SHMING. THEY DON'T MAKE'M LIKE THEY USED TO

WHA!... GUH!... I DON'T!... BUH!... YOU!... YOU!

YOU DUMB ANIMAL! YOU'RE SO STUPID, YOU DON'T KNOW WHAT YOU DID

© 1983 United Feature Syndicate, Inc.

I KNOW I DESTROYED A PRICELESS MING DYNASTY VASE AS AN OVERT EXPRESSION TO COMMUNICATE MY CONTEMPT FOR THE POLITICALLY OPPRESSIVE DOCTRINES OF THEIR EARLY 17TH CENTURY ADMINISTRATION

JIM DAVIS 7-10

7-17 JIM DAVIS

I AM ABOUT TO OUTDO MYSELF

WHAP!

© 1983 United Feature Syndicate, Inc.

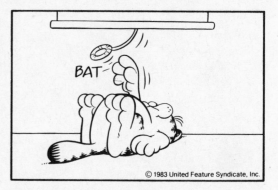

IT'S TIME YOU BOYS LEARN WHERE THE FIRE EXIT IS

IN CASE OF FIRE, GO STRAIGHT TO YOUR SWINGING PET DOOR. GOT THAT?

I'D BETTER GIVE THEM A LITTLE TEST

JIM DAVIS

9-4

FIRE!

CLEVER ME

© 1983 United Feature Syndicate, Inc.

IF YOU EAT THIS PIE, I'M GOING TO KILL YOU

© 1983 United Feature Syndicate, Inc.

GARFIELD! YOU ATE MY PIE!

JIM DAVIS   9-18

ONE OF THE GREAT CRIMINAL MINDS OF OUR TIME, I AIN'T

GARFIELD

THIS LOOKS LIKE A GOOD PLACE TO SIT AND MUSE

WHAT IS THIS THING CALLED LIFE, ODIE?

MONTAIGNE SAID, "THE VALUE OF LIFE LIES NOT IN THE LENGTH OF DAYS, BUT IN HOW WE MAKE USE OF THEM."

HOLMES SAID, "LIFE IS PAINTING A PICTURE, NOT DOING A SUM."

JAMES SAID, "BE NOT AFRAID OF LIFE. BELIEVE THAT YOUR LIFE IS WORTH LIVING, AND YOUR BELIEF WILL HELP CREATE THE FACT."

JIM DAVIS

ODIE, SOMETIMES I ENVY YOU

POO

11-6

CLICK!

WELL, LOOK WHO'S IN THE TELEVISION SET

GARFIELD IS SUCH A CLOWN

HA-HA-HA

WAH HA HA!

WAIT A MINUTE!

SOMETHING JUST OCCURRED TO ME

JIM DAVIS

© 1983 United Feature Syndicate, Inc.

11-13

MERRY CHRISTMAS, GARFIELD. I GOT YOU SOME GREAT PRESENTS!

HERE IS A RADIO CONTROLLED MOUSE...

AND A MINK SCRATCHING POST!

JIM DAVIS

PTOO

ODIE, THAT BONE IS EVERYTHING YOU OWN IN THE WORLD

12-25

IT'S THE EXPENSIVE GIFTS THAT IMPRESS ME

© 1983 United Feature Syndicate, Inc.

GARFIELD

OH BOY, WHAT A PARTY. I ATE TOO MUCH

I GOTTA GET UP AND EXERCISE. HERE I GO

OKAY, HERE I GO ON THE COUNT OF THREE... ONE, TWO, THREE AND UP!

UP... UP AND EXERCISE. COME ON, GARFIELD. YOU CAN DO IT

1-1-84   JIM DAVIS

THIS TIME I'M REALLY GOING TO DO IT. HERE GO THE LEGS LIFTING THE BODY...NOW!

THIS TIME I'M REALLY, REALLY GOING TO DO IT... ONE, TWO, THREE.... HI YA!

HAVE YOU BEEN UP TODAY, GARFIELD?

I THINK SO

1-8-84

I LOVE SACKS

I WOULDN'T KID YOU, PARNELLI. THIS HONEY WILL DO 0-60 IN 6 SECONDS FLAT

I SWEAR, SALLY, GET YOUR HEAD OUT OF THE SAND. THE SACK DRESS IS COMING BACK

I THINK I'LL STEP INTO THE ROOT CELLAR AND SEE WHAT'S FOR DINNER

OH, NO!

HELLO, MAINTENANCE? CALL THE EXTERMINATOR. MY CONDO HAS DOGS

© 1984 United Feature Syndicate, Inc.   1-22   JIM DAVIS

PLOP!

JIM DAVIS

GLUP!

© 1984 United Feature Syndicate, Inc.

2-5

PTOO
PTOO

SPLUT!

SALVAGE THE PRIDE, GARFIELD, SALVAGE THE PRIDE

GARFIELD

SMACK

LET'S PLAY!

LEAVE ME ALONE, GARFIELD

LET'S PLAY! LET'S PLAY!

OH, OKAY, WE'LL PLAY

TICKLE! TICKLE! TICKLE! TICKLE!

HA! HA! HEE! HO! HEE! HEE!

OUCH!

JIM DAVIS 3-11

I'M THROUGH PLAYING NOW

ALL RIGHT, YOU GUYS! OUTSIDE!

© 1984 United Feature Syndicate, Inc.

WHERE WERE YOU GUYS RAISED, IN A BARN? NEXT TIME USE THE DOOR

JIM DAVIS

CRASH!

THANK YOU

3-25

© 1984 United Feature Syndicate, Inc.

GARFIELD

FETCH THE STICK, ODIE!

5-13

© 1984 United Feature Syndicate, Inc.

JIM DAVIS

GARFIELD

YAWN

IT'S BEDDY-BYE TIME AGAIN

TONIGHT I THINK I'LL TAKE A DEEP BREATH, SLOWLY CLOSE MY EYES AND SAVOR THE HEAVY FEELING OF SLEEP GRADUALLY OVERTAKING MY BODY

PAT!
PAT!
PAT!

THEN AGAIN IT WOULD BE FUN TO HAVE A CUP OF COFFEE AND TOSS AND TURN FOR A COUPLE OF HOURS, THEN SLEEP 'TIL NOON

OR MAYBE I'LL RUN AROUND THE BLOCK, COLLAPSE INTO BED EXHAUSTED AND FALL ASLEEP INSTANTLY

OR I COULD WATCH THE ALL-NIGHT MOVIES ON TV UNTIL MY EYELIDS GET SO HEAVY I COULDN'T POSSIBLY HOLD THEM OPEN ANY LONGER

SIGH... SO MUCH SLEEPING TO DO AND SO FEW NIGHTS

JIM DAVIS

6-24

SCRITCH
SCRITCH

I'LL BE DARNED. THESE LABELS ARE LOOSE

IT'S THE OLD "CAT GETS THE TUNA WHILE THE OWNER GETS THE CAT FOOD" GAG

© 1984 United Feature Syndicate, Inc.

SURPRISE, GARFIELD! I FIXED US A TUNA NOODLE CASSEROLE

OH, WELL, I GUESS A HALF A SURPRISE IS BETTER THAN NONE AT ALL

7-8

JIM DAViS